Amelia Earhart

ADVENTURE IN THE SKY

Amelia Earhart

ADVENTURE IN THE SKY

by Francene Sabin
illustrated by Karen Milone

Troll Associates

Library of Congress Cataloging in Publication Data

Sabin, Francene.
    Amelia Earhart, adventure in the sky.

    Summary: A biography of an aviation pioneer
emphasizing her childhood.
      1. Earhart, Amelia, 1898-1937—Juvenile literature.
2. Air pilots—United States—Biography—Juvenile
literature. [1. Earhart, Amelia, 1898-1937.
2. Air pilots] I. Milone, Karen, ill. II. Title.
TL540.E3S23   1983   629.13'092'4 [B] [92]   82-15987
ISBN 0-89375-839-6
ISBN 0-89375-840-X (pbk.)

Amelia Earhart

ADVENTURE IN THE SKY

At the beginning of the twentieth century, little girls were supposed to be well behaved all the time. They were told to keep their dresses neat and clean. They were told to sit without fidgeting, to walk slowly, to speak softly and politely. They were supposed to be perfect little ladies.

Girls were *not* supposed to climb trees, play ball, run and jump, or get dirty. They were *not* supposed to use hammers and nails and saws. They were *not* supposed to fish or collect frogs or throw snowballs. All the things that were so much fun for little boys were considered wrong for little girls.

Most girls obeyed the rules. The few who didn't were usually punished by their parents or snubbed by their friends. But some little girls, like Amelia and Muriel Earhart, were lucky. Their mother and father felt these old-fashioned rules were silly. They believed that all children—boys *and* girls—needed plenty of exercise to grow strong and healthy.

For Amelia, born on July 24, 1898, life was fun right from the start. A bright, slim, athletic child, Amelia loved doing things from morning to night. Her sister Muriel, who was two years younger, also enjoyed rough-and-tumble play. The girls were great buddies. It didn't matter if the other children on their street in Des Moines, Iowa, laughed at them. They would laugh right back and go their own way.

Amelia and Muriel got much of their spunk from their mother, Amy Otis Earhart, who was a strong-willed, independent woman. "Too many people spend their days worrying about what they can't do," she would tell her daughters, "and about what others shouldn't do. That's a dreadful waste of time. You girls do what you feel is right, and your father and I will back you all the way."

11

Edwin Earhart shared his wife's feelings. He wanted Amelia and Muriel to be free to learn everything. Once he came home with a baseball, a baseball bat, and a basketball. That evening, he knocked the bottom out of a peach basket and nailed the frame to the barn wall. Then he laid out a small baseball field in the back yard.

In the morning, Mr. Earhart taught the girls how to pass the basketball and how to toss it

into the basket. After lunch, Mrs. Earhart joined them for a game of baseball. Each person had a turn at bat while another pitched and the other two fielded.

A few days later, while the sisters were sitting on the front steps of their house, Amelia announced, "We need more people to play baseball with us!"

"But we don't have enough players," Muriel reminded her. "Mama's reading to old Mrs. Germain down the street. And Papa won't be back till the end of the week. Baseball isn't as much fun with just two of us."

Amelia nodded gloomily. Then she brightened up. "I have a great idea," she exclaimed. "Do you know those four girls who live around the corner in the yellow house? They sit on their porch swing all the time, doing nothing. I'll bet they'd love to play baseball. Come on, let's get them!"

Muriel jumped up and clapped her hands. "Yes, right now!"

The two little girls dashed around the corner. The four Taylor sisters—Beth, Lydia, Lisa, and Caroline—were sitting in a row on the porch swing. But not for long. A short time later, they were running around the Earharts' baseball field, sliding in the dirt, and wiping sweaty faces with grimy hands. They yelled at the tops of their lungs. "Hit the ball, Beth!" "Run, Lydia, run!" and "You're out! You're out!" "I am not!"

People passing by laughed at the sight of the six little girls playing baseball. Some even stopped to watch the game and cheer the players. It was quite a scene, until Mrs. Taylor arrived. She was horrified to see her four "little ladies" playing like boys. In a voice as cold as ice, she ordered them home that very minute.

After dinner, Mrs. Earhart had visitors—several neighborhood mothers, led by Mrs. Taylor. They told Mrs. Earhart that something had to be done about Amelia before she turned all their girls into tomboys. It was a disgrace, they said. If Amelia kept on that way, none of their girls would be allowed to play with her or Muriel.

17

"I am sorry you are so upset," Mrs. Earhart said. "But I would not have my daughters change one bit. Even so, it doesn't matter. Next week we are moving away. And now I bid you all a good night."

The Earharts were leaving Des Moines because of Mr. Earhart's work. He was a lawyer for a railroad company and was away from home much of the time. Business was now taking him to California, where he would be traveling around the state for many months. He wanted Mrs. Earhart to go with him.

Amelia and Muriel were going to live with their grandparents in Atchison, Kansas. They would have liked to travel with their mother and father, but that was not possible. Amelia was six years old and ready to start school. That was exciting for her. The bright little girl had taught herself to read, and she just couldn't wait to get into a classroom and do "real work."

Judge Otis and his wife, Amelia (for whom little Amelia was named), were delighted to have their granddaughters living with them. Their two-story, brick-and-wood house had plenty of room for children. And the Otises looked forward to hearing the sounds of play and laughter that had been missing since their own children had grown up.

Amelia and Muriel also had two playmates waiting for them—Katherine and Lucy Challis, their cousins who lived in the house next door. They were just about the same ages as the Earhart girls, and they also loved to run and play. So even though Amelia and Muriel hated to see their parents leave, they couldn't be too unhappy. They had a warm, loving home and grandparents to care for them. And there were so many wonderful things to do!

Amelia easily adjusted to her new life. She was full of energy and not afraid of anything. For her first Christmas in Kansas, she asked for a sled. But she didn't want an old-fashioned girl's sled, which was slow, with thick wooden runners and a seat with a back. "I want the kind the boys use," Amelia said. "The kind the kids call a belly-whopper. With metal runners and a steering bar in front." That was just what she found under the tree on the morning of December 25, 1905.

Amelia waited eagerly for the first good snow. At last it came—a real blizzard. The next morning, Amelia, Muriel, and their cousins hurried to a hill where all the local children sledded. As soon as they got there, Amelia asked who wanted to take the first run down the snowy slope. The three girls didn't answer. They were not in a hurry to go zooming down that icy hill.

"All right, I'll do it!" Amelia said. She took a running start, threw herself onto the sled, and was off!

Girl and sled whipped down the slope, gaining speed with every second. Amelia was thrilled by the feel of the frosty air against her face and the sight of trees and houses blurring as she zipped past them. It was almost like flying!

Suddenly, Amelia saw something moving at the bottom of the hill. It was a large horse-drawn wagon. The driver, wearing earmuffs and a heavy wool hat, didn't hear or see Amelia coming at him. And there was no time for her to stop.

It was a terrifying moment. If the sled had slammed into the wagon or the horse, Amelia could have been badly hurt, even killed. But she didn't panic. With perfect timing, she steered right under the horse's belly, between its legs, and to safety on the other side.

Amelia's daring showed in other ways, too. The next summer, after a trip to the county fair, she came home excited about the roller-coaster ride. "Oh, I wish we could ride the roller coaster every day, don't you?" she asked Muriel.

Muriel agreed that would be wonderful. So did Cousins Katherine and Lucy. "Why, we could run away and work at the fair," said Katherine. "That way, we could get free rides any time we wanted."

"That's silly," Lucy told her. "Nobody would hire four kids. Besides, I like living here."

"Well, I guess we'll just have to wait till the fair comes around next year," sighed Muriel.

"No, we don't," Amelia piped up. "We'll build our own roller coaster. We'll get some boards from Grandfather's woodshed, and we'll make a track. Then we'll take the wheels off Muriel's roller skates and nail them to a square board. That will be the seat..." Still talking, she dashed out to the woodshed, blonde pigtails flying.

It took a week of work. The girls measured and sawed and nailed from dawn till sunset. Finally, they were finished. They propped the track against the woodshed. Then Amelia climbed on the roof of the shed, and Muriel handed up the board with the roller skate wheels attached to it.

"Here goes!" Amelia called out. She sat squarely on the board and pushed off. "*Owww!*" she bellowed a moment after, as she and the board slammed into the ground. "That hurts."

"Darn, I guess that's the end of our roller coaster," said Lucy.

"No, it isn't!" Amelia said. "We just made the track too short. Once it's longer, it won't have such a steep drop. I'm not going to quit now."

"Neither am I," said loyal Muriel. And she grabbed a hammer and some nails.

A few days later, the new, improved roller coaster was ready for a tryout. Amelia, of course, was the most eager to try it. This time, the ride was a great success. "I'm flying!" she cried out.

"Now it's my turn," said Katherine.

"No, mine," Lucy said.

"You'll all have lots of rides," said Amelia. And indeed they did.

Because of Amelia and Muriel's fondness for active pastimes, Mrs. Earhart bought the girls gym suits made up of baggy pants and a plain shirt. The material was sturdy, so it wouldn't tear easily, and dark blue, so the dirt didn't show too quickly. In their new gym suits, Amelia and Muriel could do almost anything—climb fences, ride horses, play football and baseball and basketball. Grandmother Otis complained that it wasn't ladylike to play such rough games. "Why, the most strenuous thing I ever did as a girl," she said, "was to roll a hoop in the public square."

The Earharts didn't agree with her. "Anything unusual is educational," Mrs. Earhart said.

Whenever Mr. Earhart was home, he took Amelia and Muriel fishing, kite-flying, or on trips to collect toads and spiders and butterflies. One time he let them stay up all night to see an eclipse of the moon. He also took them on train trips around the Midwest. "The girls learn as much from seeing new places and meeting different people as they do from going to school," he said.

Amelia attended an elementary school in Atchison, called the College Preparatory School.

She was a very good student and a fast learner. But, as ever, she did things her own way. This sometimes got her in trouble with the teachers.

One of Amelia's favorite subjects was arithmetic. She always gave the correct answers on arithmetic tests. Still, time and again, the teacher took points off her mark for not showing how she got the answers. "If you would write down all the steps in your work," the teacher told Amelia, "you would get an A on every test. You could even win the third-grade prize for arithmetic at the end of the year."

Amelia simply didn't have the patience to write down all the steps. She felt it was a waste of time. "Let some other student have the prize," she said.

When she was grown up, however, Amelia remembered how "silly and stubborn" she had been. "It doesn't make very good sense," she said, "but I probably would do things the same way if I was in school again."

Soon after Amelia finished third grade in June 1907, the Earharts moved back to Des Moines. It was there, at the Iowa State Fair, that something very wonderful happened in Amelia's life. She saw an airplane for the first time. It had two wings, one over the other, and a large wooden propeller. The pilot sat between the wings, in front of a small motor. It wasn't much to look at—just some pieces of wood and canvas held together by wire. But what counted most was what the airplane could do!

All of her life Amelia remembered when the pilot pulled a big pair of goggles over his eyes. He signaled to a friend to start the propeller. Moments later, the motor sputtered to life, and the plane began to move. It rolled slowly over the grassy field, then lifted into the air. Amelia's heart rose with it. The date was July 24—Amelia's ninth birthday—and she couldn't have asked for a finer present!

Today, children see airplanes all the time, and many children have taken trips in one. But back in 1907, a flying machine was a rare sight, indeed! Only four years before, the Wright brothers had flown a plane for the first time in history. Nobody knew yet what to do with the new invention except to show it off at fairs and celebrations. None of that mattered to nine-year-old Amelia. She felt that flying was the most beautiful thing she could imagine.

During the next few years, Amelia didn't see another plane or think much about flying. She continued to be a good student in school. She loved to read and spent hours at the library. Every kind of book was interesting to her— novels, adventure stories, books about the lives of important people, about science, geography, history, and art.

Amelia wanted to learn all there was to know, so she decided to read her way through the local library. She started at one end of the shelves of books, planning to keep reading until she reached the other end.

Of course, Amelia never completed her plan. There were simply too many other things to do—like tennis, horseback riding, swimming, and other sports. And she had to learn nearly all of these things on her own because, in those days, girls were not taught to compete at sports.

All through her life, Amelia was annoyed that she was never as good an athlete as she wanted to be. "Exercise of all kinds gave me intense pleasure," she said. "I might have been more skillful and graceful if I had learned the correct form in athletics. But I couldn't get any instruction, so I just played and acquired a lot of bad habits."

38

Today, girls are admired for being fine athletes. But that wasn't the case in the early 1900s. The tall, slim, competitive Amelia was too different to be popular with her classmates. She was respected for her intelligence and skills, but was not often invited to parties and dances.

Amelia did want to be liked by the other teenagers at school—but not if she had to pretend to be somebody she wasn't. She didn't faint or scream at the sight of a mouse, and she wasn't going to act frightened. She wasn't comfortable in frilly dresses. Needlework wasn't as interesting to her as astronomy. "For better or worse," she said to Muriel, "this is who I am. And this is who I'll always be."

Through her high-school years, Amelia continued to be a loner. When she graduated, the inscription under her yearbook picture read: "Amelia Earhart, the girl who walks alone." It was the price she paid for being different—but she *knew* it was worth it!

In 1916, Amelia went to visit Muriel, who was going to school in Toronto, Canada. While there, Amelia saw many wounded soldiers. They were Canadians who had been hurt in the First World War.

"I must do something to help," Amelia told her sister. The very next day, she went to work as a nurse's aide in a military hospital. The patients liked her immediately. All the things that had made her a loner before—independence,

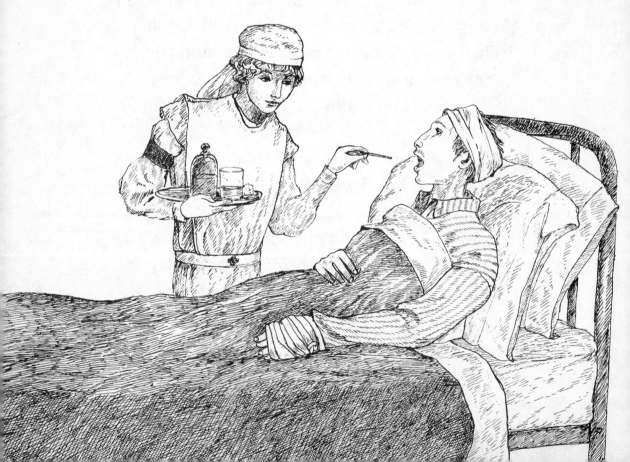

willingness to do any job, fearlessness, and the direct way she talked to people—made her a success now.

On a day off from her work at the hospital, eighteen-year-old Amelia went to a nearby airfield with a friend. It was many years since she had seen an airplane fly, and what she saw now thrilled her. The new planes were better built and could fly faster and farther. The pilots put their aircraft through all sorts of stunts—dives and rolls and loops.

Amelia watched, breathless. "I must learn to fly," she promised herself. "I must!"

Four years later, Amelia kept that promise. In 1920, when the Earharts were living in Long Beach, California, Amelia went to see an air show. There she met Frank Hawks, a pilot who was willing to take her for a short flight. He even let her handle the controls for a few minutes. It was everything she had ever dreamed it would be.

To pay for flying lessons, Amelia took a job with the telephone company. She worked during the week and spent her weekend at the airfield. Her teacher was Neta Snook, one of America's first women fliers. "Snookie" was a demanding teacher, who insisted that Amelia learn everything there was to know about planes and flying. She had the eager student learn to take apart the engine, oil it, and put it together again.

Amelia also learned how to read the instrument panel and how to fly in different kinds of weather, in daylight and in darkness. Not until she had done all this, and had logged many hours of airtime, was she ready to fly alone. Except for a slightly bumpy landing, her first solo flight was perfect. She was a pilot!

In the years that followed, Amelia Earhart became the world's greatest female flier. She set dozens of speed and altitude records. She was the first woman to fly alone across the Atlantic Ocean. She won many honors, medals, and decorations from countries all around the world.

Amelia was the first pilot—male or female—to fly solo from Hawaii to California; from California to Mexico City; from Mexico City to Newark, New Jersey. She inspired thousands of people to take up flying. As a writer and public speaker, she made millions of friends for aviation. But she was happiest when she was up in the sky, flying.

Amelia Earhart became rich, successful, and famous. She had a happy marriage and a full life.

Yet even with all this, there was one special goal that she wanted to reach—to be the first pilot to circle the globe at the equator. Then she could say she had flown farther in one trip than anyone in history.

On the morning of June 1, 1937, Amelia and navigator Fred Noonan took off from Miami, Florida, on the first leg of their round-the-world flight. They flew south to Puerto Rico, then to South America. After that, they headed east, over the South Atlantic on their way to Africa.

The flight soared on successfully for 22,000 miles, until July 1. On that day, Amelia took off from New Guinea, in the South Pacific. She was

beginning the longest nonstop leg of the flight—
2,556 miles to Howland, another Pacific island.
She never arrived.

Somewhere over the vast Pacific Ocean, the
plane vanished. For weeks, it was hoped that
Amelia Earhart and Fred Noonan were alive,
drifting on a raft somewhere at sea. Search planes
and ships were sent out, but they could not find a
trace of the plane or its crew.

Over the years, a number of people have come forward with ideas about what happened to the heroic flier. Some say she survived and went to live on a small island. Some say she was captured by Japanese soldiers on an island being used as a military base. But there has never been any proof of these—or any other—stories.

Today, most people believe that Amelia's plane crashed into the ocean and that she died instantly. Whatever her fate, the legacy of her courage and spirit survives. The name of Amelia Earhart lives on as one of America's pioneers of aviation.